My Train is On Schedule

By Márquez Price

Table of Contents

Commonplace

Love is war,

war is love—

The thrills and throes serve as camouflage for one another.

The victor seeks to deny the memory of the fallen,

but the fallen will rise in another foe.

Patois

They love the phonetics,

heard it leap from my tongue of patois —

eavesdrop of the marauder.

Scraps they gave us as slaves,

We converted to soul food.

We didn't eat that way —

When Negus was king,

And God was NGR.

Pillaged resources from the land,

Beat of the drum,

The mother tongue —

Our language was subsequent.

Confuse a hard R with an endearing A.

Not your Nigger,

Nor ya nigga.

Heart Chakra

There's been a groundswell of opposition to your existence,

but I found you —

like the first time I tasted Baklava.

Between Marvin,

and Sinatra record sleeves —

you danced across tile flooring,

and vinyl sound —

in a vessel of woman to pique the possibility of love.

Again.

Prickly Pear Juice

He watched gravity grovel at her gait —

with cinnamon skin tone and gangly limbs.

Largesse for gratuity,

He went back daily to the café not for what she served on his plate —

but what she filled his heart with.

10 Second Count

Misfortune,

you knew I'd find the bristles—

to sweep shards after the impact from hurt you gave me,

and pocket those pieces of hardship.

Put 'em back together,

and make 'em work.

Like a pittance for school lunch,

from wrinkled dollars—

unearthed from the pits of a struggling mother's purse,

that mouths of vending machines spurn.

By hook or by crook,

I persevered.

I called my power back to me—

Tribulation,

you knew.

Family Tree

They were 10 poor kids from Gary, Indiana —

waiting for visitors with loose pockets to leave —

so that they could scrounge underneath cushions.

Through crevices of an old couch for shiny coins,

for a pot of burnt beans.

Stirred to quiet echoed hunger from hollow bellies —

so that we,

their children,

could tell you how they survived.

Early Duties

Sunshine squeezes through loosened blinds —
gleam on your neck,
from a morning peeled eye.
Saturday morning.
Let the yard wait —
tools strewn on top of dirt,
and weeds protruding like whisks from broom handles.
You are where I begin my work.

Uncle Randle

I remember catching his hand to shake it--

unbeknownst to the fact that he was left-handed,

because of the dexterity of his right hand.

He showed me how to look at both sides--

of the spectrum in life,

and ambidexterity.

From the future and back

The meteor with her hair pulled back into a ponytail,
and tourmaline black eyes.

Archeologists will excavate the impact your love had on me
thousands of years from now.

Combat

I thought she was crazy —

A loose term mechanized to dismiss,

And defend what I didn't understand.

Snappin' her fingers,

Raisin' her voice,

and conjuring accusations from a wobbly perception.

I later realized she wasn't toxic.

She was trying to communicate that she had been traumatized —

and that convoluted,

hard armor was a covering —

Constructed to protect a world within that a little girl had seen betrayed too many times,

with missiles ready to launch whenever her buttons were pushed.

Perspective

Being a pallbearer in the morning,

and a best man later that night,

was my lesson of living in the present.

Beauty

Ephemeral beauty is physical,

like the flavor of that cheap bubblegum we chewed from the ice cream truck as kids.

Everlasting beauty is amorphous —

like the child's imagination,

coloring outside of the lines.

Moons

My sister burned my neck with a curling iron,

as I teased about her weight in the bathroom when we were kids.

I was insensitive to how the girlfriends I had could have mood swings,

and I had to accept it,

every month for an unpredicted number of days.

The helplessness I felt,

the first time my niece experienced her menstrual cycle,

was ineffable.

It rearranged my empathy.

Time Travel

I never saw him lollygag —

for his urgency was rooted in his knowing that we are once a man,

and twice a child —

during the physical dash below the epitaph as men.

Meditation

Sometimes I live in my head,

and your mind is not your friend —

until I discovered that mindfulness is the intermediary between space,

and thoughts.

Camaraderie

The four of them are meant to celebrate life —

through art,

music,

humanity,

and friendship.

They are the four corners of a compass that know where to meet on a common force of magnetism.

Medicine

It wasn't the shamans in Peru,

rituals,

or the clairvoyant —

that made him to realize that she wasn't a femme fatal.

He made himself susceptible to getting hurt,

by abandoning his love of self.

Uncle Raymond

"Engaging conversationalist,

Intellectual pugilist—

Raymond could defense,

shuffle,

and counter,

through the boxing ring canvas of your mind."

Patterns

The birds and bees talk with my nephew will go like this:

Your grandfather abandoning your father,

was not your fault.

Your father abandoning you,

was not your fault.

The generational pattern,

is your responsibility to break.

Divine Intervention

You are necessary

the last words my uncle spoke to me before he died.

His premonition sat itself at the vestibule of my mind,

And served as the mettle I'd need,

for what awaited me around the corner.

Transitioning gave him access to this dimension,

and the next.

Football Numbers

I'll never forget the look you gave me —

after the robe threw down his gavel,

and spoke 21 years of your future behind bars.

So,

now I write words between lines,

sealed in envelopes,

hoping you can live vicariously through my freedom.

Queen Bee

My grandmother was five foot nothing.

She would *give all 160 of the pounds* she weighed if you got on her bad side.

A mathematical wizard,

she'd charge 25 cents on the dollar to a borrower.

She could crack walnuts with her bare hands–

and knock a man out with her emerald green eyes,

or fists.

She could produce the skill of culinary from whatever was available,

never sharing her unwritten recipes.

You had to wash your hands before you entered her kitchen,

but she'd sit me —

and my filthy,

backyard-coated hands right next to the sink,

and let me reach into that coveted jar.

The best chocolate chip cookies to ever dissolve in a mouth.

Her secret act of kindness to a cub was as sweet as honeycomb.

She spent 90 months of her life carrying 10 children.

She was *a breeding woman,*

as she said,

"the *Queen Bee,*

Mattie C,

Buzzing around her hive."

Financial Literacy

Old man Perry would pull up to the barbershop in his Caddy.

Slide it next to the slab of concrete,

and park it.

Cab Calloway swagger—

loud suit,

zoot wool felt fedora hat on tilt,

with his grey hair matted down the sides like cardigan wool.

Pulled out a fist full of folded scratch,

with the gold cash clip,

and handed me a few greenbacks.

"Don't spend all that in one place, baby. It takes some to make some."

He was planting seeds,

for me to rake leaves later,

from my own money tree.

9 Ether

Melanated him,

and Melanated her.

Shea butter scented fingertips,

his head in her lap.

Sacred sessions every weekend by the futon with the mahogany frame,

sage burning.

Washed the scalp underneath his coiled crown —

reminded him of Orion's belt,

and orishas.

Gave him herbal remedies,

sea buckthorn,

and black seed oil.

Showed him how to eat better —

soursop,

celery,

almonds,

jackfruit,

and dark chocolate.

Twisted hair on a tender head,

designs braided down to the follicles.

Kundalini exchange —

she carried their love ¾ of a solar return,

and birthed a nine ether being.

Rumpelstiltskin muse

Aesthetics —

like the first time I saw her,

art in motion.

Euphonious —

like the first time I heard her voice.

Her essence —

is either indelible,

or spinning like a wheel —

interlacing years to gold that never loses its luster.

My People

My people are the Khoisan —

I was part of the largest group of humans on earth.

My people are the Dogon —

I have boundless knowledge of stars,

Universal frame is my body.

My people are powerful,

Like the Songhai empire.

My people advanced regions of Europe in every way,

Like the pedagogy of the Black Moors.

My people built the pyramids —

They say aliens built them,

We are the aliens.

My people are remembering who they are —

They thought we would forget.

Cousin Derrick

The witticisms,

made us wheeze with laughter.

A debonair Southern style,

and the charisma that could palm an entire lineage was unparalleled.

Never physically been in an earthquake,

but the news received about you passing away was an epicenter of loss.

From Southern drawl to a dial tone,

sometimes the inconvenience of life doesn't allow you to say good-bye to a family member.

Swim Lessons

We tried to swim.

Our bodies descended into the Atlantic,

tossed from floating dungeons,

sustenance for trailing sharks.

They fire hosed our flesh when we demanded rights,

no ointment—

for the lattice wound on our backs,

a reverberating whip that sang,

and cut through our psyche for a perpetual sting.

We don't like to swim.

It evokes memory of ships,

and shores.

Her

Your aura,
kaleidoscopic.
The pull of your energy,
Gravitational.
Spoken from a Santeria reading,
I heard I'd walk beside you upon Santorini lava pebbles.
and we did.

Protection

The moxie he wore was too baggy for his diminutive stature.

A clicking noise in his pocket,

he pulled out,

and pointed at me.

Deuce deuce in his grip,

froze me like a car acquiescing to the whim of a stop light at an intersection.

The remorse underneath his hooded eyes mimicked a mannequin.

He was showing me that his gun was his God,

and my life was in his hands.

Be prey,

or pray,

at fifteen —

the gun lodged in my pants as my new religion thereafter.

Abundance

We struggle with isolation,

because we are afraid to spend time with the person that we will spend the most time with,

during our entire lives.

Ourselves.

The paradox is that when you go within,

you discover that you are not alone.

Skin Deep

My quintessential mother.

She is a heart person,

with esoteric usage of altruism.

She served as the portal for me to come here,

her image is the only one that will ever be inked on my skin.

Hero

The alpha man's man.

He doesn't waste time chewin' the fat with you,

and if you've ever walked beside him,

you'd better lift your knees in stride to keep up with his boxer's bop.

He showed me there's no need to be perfect when you're consistent,

and true to yourself.

I've never wasted time in appreciating him —

like Furious Styles,

I could have been Doughboy,

or Ricky.

Boyz in a hood my old man survived —

so many fatherless boys disavowed by men who looked just like them,

derelict in their parental duties.

They were around the corner,

and across the street,

He took me to the beach —

where waves reached for our heels,

and receded back into existential wonder-

moments crystallized in time,

like the sand beneath our feet,

following his lead,

footprints that led me to become the man I am now.

My Father.

Ho'oponopono

I love you.

I'm sorry.

Please Forgive me.

And thank you.

A Hawaiian practice.

Four phrases I speak to myself,

And the ones I love,

When on the brink of destruction.

Honey

My mother used to call my father "honey" when I was little,

but to me,

honey was something you put on bread.

My eureka moments occurred —

when you poured bleach down the drain so my sink wouldn't stink,

and introduced me to Chai tea with milk to drink —

when you took scissors,

and cut a piece of cactus from your front yard,

to squeeze,

and apply aloe vera to the wound on my skin.

From the first time I met you that night,

it felt like a moonlight tryst.

This must be the place

 like talking heads.

The familiarity made me reexamine reincarnation.

You were sweet as,

Honey.

Energy

Man said he was God in his own image to establish dominion over nature.

Woman said she was Goddess to neutralize the bane of misogyny.

The indigenous man said the land was God.

The conquering man said the savior was white but forgot the scripture didn't match the description.

The original man said he was the true and living God in the flesh.

The atheist said the rest were trying to personify themselves as deities and were too squeamish to embrace death.

Death said it is undefeated and life gets the glory.

Life said death is jealous because its prominent feature is the moment.

Energy said, "I am forever."

Star Gazing

We stare into space during the night,
until I speak Kama Sutra to each,
and every star,
placed on your celestial body.

Salutations

I remember having intuitions of your arrival —

Delivered often like a gazette,

Of a spirit that would gambol like a gazelle,

Into a habitat roamed in times,

Before and again,

Together.

Black folks

We fight for inner peace,

every day,

And we fight for the rights of our people,

every day.

Our mental,

emotional,

and spiritual health is crucial.

Wake up from Ashwagandha aided sleep,

soak in Epsom salt,

Swill kombucha,

Burn nag champa,

and light a spliff with the same match to smoke for breakfast —

just to cope with approaching the PTSD of great-grand generations.

If the propensity of our species is to survive,

we are the exemplar.

Prayer

My mama prays every night,

because she knows I won't look to the sky.

Rather I,

will summon Madison Washington,

and Nat Turner,

to fight back,

but I pray for her too—

for a mother's worry,

of her only son,

needs peace.

Tipping bottles

We poured out liquor,

for the ones gone before our time on the surface,

with a subconscious knowing underneath,

of our connection to libation offerings to our ancestors.

Elevators

We are Gods and Goddesses,

As children in costumes,

Masquerading as adults —

Bumping up against each other,

With primal energies,

Fluctuating tiers,

Between lower vibration,

And our higher selves,

Of human experience.

Ambivalent

Addicted to you one minute,

Couldn't stand you the next,

Hypnotic.

Tongue-fu,

Verbal fights,

And 69 maneuvers hours later in the same dojo.

Just raw —

In temperament,

And intercourse,

Toxic.

You got a kick out of screaming on me,

Until I snapped and said things too strong for levies to yield —

Springing tears from your eyes,

Accompanied by a deranged smile,

You've snapped too,

And we've arrived at a place where our arousal towards each other,

Is sadistic,

And twisted —

Where bright lights are blinding,

The sound of loud music overrides logic,

And man's weakness for the physical exacts punitive measures,

By way of karmic lessons repeated,

For us both,

And my judgment is flawed in being present while you work,

At the strip club.

Overcast

Haystack made from a pile of used needles,

a man made a broom out of a sweater to sweep them,

Hefty bag full of his belongings.

decriminalized substance abuse,

and the opiate epidemic tandem,

for a passerby to roll down the street,

and see usage displayed openly,

I'm looking to see where the kids play in the park.

The scenery is commotion.

A naked man murmuring to himself,

dancing,

and darting,

in between puddles of trash—

the energy of his spirit reverberates from an exhausted body,

trying to break free from the routine of aimless wandering,

in and out of buildings looking for something to eat.

A woman trailing a man,

yelling her disappointments to a deaf ear.

The dogs are dejected—

Sunken eyes with a sullen sky,

It rains in Portland,

all the time,

They're just trying to cope.

Shaman

Through ambient sound,

And a trance,

She spoke —

We women have the immense ability to love a being,

That hijacks our bodies,

And sucks our nutrients before we can get them.

We are chemically geared to allow that being to explode into this world,

Through seemingly impossible spaces,

And then everything in us is geared to love that being —

No matter if they don't let you sleep for a year,

Cry all day,

And then turn into teenagers who disregard.

We are made to not leave.

Biologically,

Men are not geared for staying through such things so,

Show me a man's relationship with his mother,

And I'll show you his ability to treat a woman.

Harbinger

I am angry.

Ozone layer depletion,

gas emissions from transportation,

powered by oil rigs.

Emaciated polar bears cling to melting glacier caps,

an evanescent bee population-

they pollinate the produce in your grocery stores.

Potential nuclear warfare between countries has marred the totality of human spirit,

love and fear cannot occupy the same space at the same time.

The error of your ways,

and generations before you,

have become the incarnation of hubris that eschews its responsibility to coexist with me,

as inhabitants.

A butterfly,

no bigger than your palm.

Brachiosaurus,

larger than the house you sleep in,

and the turtle,

walking deliberately through time,

all here long before you.

I am angry.

The ruination of ecosystems,

people are perishing,

endangered species,

an extinction level event is slated to take place from your written hands of apathy.

You have omitted the suffering of the world,

cries from the crestfallen are muffled.

Deforestation,

ask the trees —

3.1 trillion of them,

422 per person.

They absorb the air,

their lungs breathe in carbon dioxide,

and with the help of the sun,

the carbon stays in the trees,

Oxygen gets released,

this is how you breathe.

You discard plastic bottles in excess on California beaches,

the trash that clogs oceanic gyres,

circulating ocean water,

impacting all life.

One organism,

no division.

To view me from space would usher in an epiphany.

Everything that exists within the universe —

the elements,

exists within you,

and I,

but I am angry.

You have made information available to the touch,

and technology at your fingertips-

excuses equal nil.

Your United Nations predicted disaster if global warming was not checked over 30 years ago,

1989.

They said entire nations could be washed off the face of earth by rising sea levels,

if the global warming trend was not reversed by 2000.

It's 2020,

and your commander-in-chief has the audacity to profess fake news.

I see no alarm in you.

I sent smoke signals into the atmosphere from the Amazon rainforest,

and Sub-Saharan Africa terrain ablaze.

I rattled Fukushima plants in Japan,

spilling nuclear waste that will alter cells in your bodies from the fish you eat.

You named me Katrina when I broke the levees in New Orleans.

I shook the ground,

snapping trees like toothpicks,

and crumbling buildings like paper in Port-au-Prince.

But,

in your green God you trust,

there is no premium on my repair —

Annuit coeptis,

an ideal providence would favor the undertakings of all,

not one.

Novus ordo seclorum,

the new order of the ages is not possible without me.

Without you,

I am capable of thriving.

I will regenerate.

Your children come through you,

but not from you.

They are watching you.

Your behavior of yesterday,

will thwart their tomorrow,

if you do not guide them today,

in the face of finite disappointment,

they will exercise infinite hope,

to save me,

the planet.

The Shift

It appeared unseen out of thin air,

flu-like and the world started shutting down.

Impaired is the vision once used to see sunshine,

now blotted out by fear.

There's-there's-there's no way this is happening,

denial steps forward,

the extrapolation of what is at hand steps back.

Schumann resonances lit up—

dolphins started swimming near the coasts of Italy,

deer roamed free in the streets of Japan,

monkeys in Thailand,

amazing pollution cuts occurred in China—

The planet breathed bluer skies through respiration,

unimpeded by our generated emissions.

Nature is showing us that it has no timetable,

we became the animals in a zoo to a place we lease,

and do not own.

Reality has arrived,

and we're pointing fingers.

Acceptance reclines back in a seat knowing our disbelief will
turn weary.

We grew impatient.

The young are shielded by their youth,

those with seniority blame the young for the spread —

As the youth disregard tomorrow for now with limited memories of yesterday,

and elders hold onto now in appreciation of time through the lens of yesterday,

and hope for tomorrow.

We're all pathologizing each other —

Sofa physicians,

asymptomatic,

handshakes and hugs are treated like Trojan horses on the shores of our precautionary measures.

A sneeze will get you a scarlet letter in a public that will diagnose your symptoms.

It's become an infodemic,

someone said plandemic on social media.

A vaccine volley between altruism,

and individualism,

Conspiracy vs science grapple for your choice of dogma.

Insomnia,

I'm chewing on valerian root for sleep.

Surging cases with variants,

and mutations after curfews are lifted.

Protesting lockdowns to go outside in search of relic 2019.

My homeboy serving a prison bid gave me perspective from his cell on a phone call,

while the rest of us feel like we're doing time.

I'm remembering that study about solitary confinement-

how it'll make your psychological strings snap when human contact,

and sunlight are taken away.

we stared gorging ourselves for comfort,

80% will be diabetic in 10 years.

Someone grabbed the farm and shook it,

we're aimless ants searching for the queen of purpose.

They hunted and ran down a man who looked just like me —

shot him down as he viscerally fought back to survive.

Saddled with rage,

and wishing someone would,

I'm anxious to throw from the shoulders,

and engage in hand-to-hand combat.

The anger persists,

and is interwoven with paranoia-

I'm at the gun store buying a chrome .357 magnum with the rubber grip.

He was jogging,

I'm running now with an instrument of protection tucked in my shorts,

That I thought I only had to reach under the seat of my car for when an intruder appears —

I'm not staying safe,

I'm staying dangerous.

We all we got.

May the ancestors guide me in peace,

or in war.

I saw a cop kneel on the neck of another man who looks like me,

8 min and 46 seconds,

before he called for his mother and died.

A zeitgeist deployed from quarantine,

we're not just marching,

a tantrum known to the powerful —

as one easily outwaited.

Armed with information,

we hold ammunition in our ideas,

with subsequent actions towards immediate change.

Looting,

protesting,

and rioting —

depends on displacement,

survival,

and catharsis —

three interchangeable pairs shuffled in a shell game by media outlets.

We acted out in solidarity,

laughing like,

you know the woopty woop woop to recap the highlights —

frolic for the forgotten.

Stimulus checks,

and one big litmus test,

vitriol revealed in the comments online.

Babel through masks to protect us from a virus at the grocery store,

but our greed swiped supplies faster than they could be stocked.

The poor are marginalized more,

and the homeless are more visible,

as they've been brought courtside to a game that we have denied their participation in.

Depression and isolation ran a two-on-one fast break on many,

forcing them to be backpedaled into the bleachers of despair.

For the first time in my life,

I haven't touched a basketball in days,

weeks,

months.

fires burning in the mountains,

fires burning in the streets.

I'm watching V for Vendetta for the first time in years,

and this time it feels like the movie is watching me.

Unemployment skyrockets.

The plight of workers became essential to our survival.

Pandemic brain fog,

days become enmeshed,

and we are mired in a desolate world of thoughts.

True colors emerged —

black,

white,

and political spectrum.

The leader of the free world made it obvious for the world to see,

that denial can no longer Trump the fact that this country is divided.

A tipping point desecrated the Capitol,

privilege escaped with impunity,

soft targets are being terrorized again for shootings.

Religious zealots were born,

others abandoned their religion.

Some got into the best shape of their lives without a gym,

Depression continues to loom monstrously for many.

I'm burning two palo santo sticks at once,

.357 still on my lap.

Some lost businesses,

others improved tax brackets.

People are moving from LA to Texas,

and New York to Miami.

The economy is starting to boom,

and the stock market is more prosperous than volatile for those willing to take risks.

Demand is high for budgeting

and saving—

Supply looks like developing multiple streams of income.

I'm mastering financial literacy.

Some were hooked up to respirators in the hospital,

others bounced back after 72 hours of resting.

Those coping through an Epicurean lifestyle,

lack the empathy needed for those grieving the loss of loved ones.

I'm taking black seed oil,

and Epsom salt baths.

My meditation is deeper—

Chi,

Prana,

and Ra.

Just breathe.

The news has us engrossed by the numbers,

tethered to a death toll that has couched our mortality right next to us while we watch.

I know for certain I want kids,

and get married—

Anxieties of a single man I've never felt before.

The voice within affirms my train is on schedule,

the fret assuages.

One thing is certain,

this pandemic doesn't discriminate.

I'm eating consciously.

You are what you eat,

and the company you keep,

both determining your greatest wealth —

health.

Some made babies in marital bliss.

Some discovered they couldn't live with their spouse when they met them for the first time,

shaking hands with familiarity long enough to breed a new relationship of contempt.

Nurses saw bodies get stiff while working graveyard shifts.

Some of my friends overdosed,

some put the bottle down for good.

I've hiked every mountain in the Southwest.

I worked remote,

then went back into the office for human interaction.

Temperature guns and social distancing,

I've watched every movie on Netflix.

I'm reading a book a week.

I bought a new laptop.

I'm back writing.

Facetime,

and Zoom have kept our loved ones in touch through a keyboard.

Quietude has taken up space in the mind for some,

and they have reconnected with themselves.

Others are bored,

unable to spend time with themselves.

What is most important in life resurfaces,

my priorities are intact.

Egos are starting to die.

Tough facades are no longer impenetrable,

and my spirit frequents places where forever resides,

hurdling each impasse separating me,

and the people my love will never cease to envelop.

I've forgiven myself,

for not knowing what I didn't know until I went through it,

and am open to all.

I engage with my purpose.

I set intentions by writing them down-

Courage words are of solitude thoughts.

Affirmations,

I am,

no longer what no longer serves me,

if not in alignment,

focus on evolution,

We can meet there.

My hope is that we all realize en masse that we are all connected deeply.

The burning continues to persist,

as does my optimism.

There is ancient knowledge in the wind,

and when the world feels a little ill —

I close my eyes and hear it whisper,

love is the panacea.

Nebula

Her countenance was misery wrapped in cellophane.

In the evenings,

punching whims,

and caterwaul echoed from your parent's room,

and somehow,

you were punished with disdain by your mother as a result
of resembling your father.

A life of toil in construction manufactured his grimy,

calloused hands.

The Vietnam vet ruminated the throes of war daily —

The jungle,

M16's,

machetes,

and shrapnel.

Grenades,

and mines.

Combat boots with squishy soles that trudged through rain
drenched terrain,

soaked fatigues.

Insect repellent versus unmerciful mosquitoes.

The providential M1 helmet with the bullet lodged in it,

the faces of the men he killed spliced with the faces of his
fallen comrades —

a rope that would inextricably knot his pain,

and lasso the wife and kids of his future into his torture chamber.

Your father talked about combat all the time.

Your father's caprice commandeered your childhood joy,

the moment he stepped into the house so,

you learned reconnaissance was pivotal in navigating the battleground you knew as home.

Make it to the bedroom.

Others at school saw you as the quiet oddity with tattered clothes,

and matted hair,

but the only white boy in the neighborhood,

and I,

became fast friends on the school bus.

Burgundy bruises blotched on your skin after nights of your father's drunken outbursts,

and I knew why you wore flannel long sleeved shirts in the spring.

When the wheels on the bus screeched to drop you off at home,

the consternation ran wild in your eyes,

and our unspoken communication commenced —

make it to the bedroom.

The first time I saw him strike you,

a running jump kick to the jaw that sent you careening to the ground.

I don't know if I was more alarmed at your reaction to what seemed routine, or the calmness of his suggestion that I head home after he struck you.

Slippery charm,

accompanied by murky disposition is always best discerned by a child's radar,

and I picked up on your father's signal.

A quagmire became my routine —

witnessing him hit you oftentimes,

but tell naught out of fear that he'd do more.

One day I found myself in the principal's office,

sitting across from her and a police officer-

my secret turned into disclosure by proximity to your plight.

Two nights later a rock sailed through my bedroom window.

As I cautiously stepped half asleep over broken glass in the dark to turn on the light,

your father's pick-up truck engine confessed that a rock was his retaliation,

for what I had divulged at school.

A month later you became a permanent absentee from school.

The "For Sale" sign that stood at the bottom of your driveway cemented my friend's departure.

In an unforeseeable future,

serendipity would place a vacationing man,

and a homeless man in the seat of an encounter.

Coming of age would be different for one of the friends.

It included a path that would twist,

and turn through continued abuse,

runaways,

dropouts,

fringe social milieu interactions,

graduations,

and drowning in bottles his father had gone adrift in.

His spirit still congenial,

and unbroken,

my friend now stood in front of me,

eerily resembling his father 20 years since the last time I saw him.

He had left a corporate life behind to live freely,

and homeless along the beach where the flashing tides reach,

and recede as people often do in life yet some,

like nebula,

remain in memory long after their impact.

My Brother's Keeper

We were inner-city adolescent kings,

inseparable,

you were the brother that I never had.

You grew up in a neighborhood that my father survived to provide me with a better life.

Entrenched by trepidation,

the streets were pathways to violence,

and prison cells.

The cornerstone was a pharmaceutical rock,

manufactured in dilapidated houses for peddler profit,

that sent addicts on aimless journeys.

Red and blue lights danced to the song of sirens,

and ears became attuned to what type of guns were being shot at rival gangs,

while hysterical dogs barked at wafting apparitions that once occupied the neighborhood.

Go to the park,

and select one of two options —

Hone your skills on the basketball court,

by pouring your soul into an iron rim with chained nets,

or sell it to the luck thrown in dice,

by them boys who brandished guns for blue paisley printed flag affiliation.

Gazelle lean,

brown hare speed,

and praying mantis limbs —

your movement seemed immortally enhanced,

as if the athletic Gods nourished you with ambrosia at birth.

We ran in the backcourt together,

where our Siamese twin chemistry bestowed repetitive sequences like —

rebound,

outlet,

dribble,

dribble,

mid-air pass,

and dunks in two- man fast break with zoom speed-

that left five opposing defenders mired in pedestrian bewilderment.

We played Rikki-Tikki-Tavi one- on- one games with orchestrated shoe screeches,

snapping nets,

and wooden thumped floors,

that shot darting echoes throughout a hallowed gymnasium,

that we designated as our black boy sanctuary.

We'd go to the same shop,

same barber,

and get the same haircut on our same birthday,

before going to the same mall,

to buy the same shoes,

to walk to the same theater,

to watch the same movie,

with the same two girls who were best friends like us.

But things change when struggle stays the same.

Your grandparents,

Miss Victoria in the kitchen,

and Howard working the graveyard shift wasn't enough to feed,

or refuge in a house full of grandkids as you found your niche in the streets.

I transferred schools,

and you soon dropped out of school.

Hard knock life adaptations,

and the need for bare essentials ensued so the choice was made—

Crip family,

blue bandana,

gun tucked in the waist,

and crack capsules pocketed to distribute to addicts who classified as your capitalistic clientele.

The black father guiding me in the front,

flanked by a mother's love,

pointed me in the right direction,

but survivor's guilt followed me as I saw you being left by the wayside.

By the time I was graduating college,

you had watched gun violence,

and death,

wrest your brother,

and many other homeboys away.

You spent the most quality time in one year as you ever had with your father,

as each other's cellmate in prison,

and left prison only see another street disciple from the 'hood enter a correctional facility,

to serve a lifetime sentence.

His abode,

a steal bedstead holding a mattress,

a one-piece sink,

and toilet assembled of welded,

stainless steel,

and a door with a small safety glass window with a metal flap that opens to serve meals.

As men now,

we run into each other at the same barbershop,

but things aren't the same.

Your eyes are sunken,

puffed by bags that hold a beady trance.

The hair on your head is sparse,

and the skin on your face has undergone metamorphic strain to resemble a man who looks exhausted,

and weathered.

The homies you once ran with are locked up,

still clinging to cyclical gang ties,

or are resting in the cemetery silence —

A silence you're left with to wander the same streets,

with no home,

and an addiction to a drug you once sold.

We see each other,

and the love between us remains.

You're slumped against the barber's chair,

fatigued,

but still speak through your eyes when you see me with a gleaming smile.

I hand our barber twenty dollars and kneel down to hug you,

"I love you, brotha."

I leave the barbershop,

trailed by the shadow of worry that I may have seen you for the last time.

The morning

Like saucers in the night,

what you throw to the universe,

the universe will frisbee back.

Karma eventually reveals what was once hidden,

and my karma was to temporarily lose what I once hid,

for me to see I was doing wrong,

but what is written in the stars,

is infinite,

and never lost.

I come from a father who holds grudges,

because a black man must keep his guard up for survival,

and a mother who forgives fast,

because a black woman birthed a civilization that forgot
her —

and after they fought,

silence would loom for days between them,

and a game of tag would ensue between me,

and anxiety.

Silent treatment made me uneasy,

even just experiencing it with observation.

It didn't occur to me until I attempted to speak to others
from a silenced voice,

that the child in me was being triggered.

It taught me not to add anger to things taken personal for equaled revenge,

because being vindictive to teach a lesson only makes us students in the process —

it's all just feelings,

compounded when applying to someone you love.

Recognize the error of your ways,

apologize,

grow from your mistakes,

forgive.

Tell the truth,

say no when needed for boundaries,

and ask for what you want.

Lessons I received from healing,

not from blame for anyone else.

I was driven never to be a man hardened with pain,

ducking conversations about uncomfortable topics,

because he never learned to speak it,

scared of the notion that it's over if a woman sees her man showing weakness.

My understanding of cheating was found within the boundaries of what a woman defines it as,

because a man will find the elasticity in boundaries to stretch them —

like,

a physical encounter with another woman is OK if you and I are just talking, and if we are exclusive in seeing each other then that grants leeway if we have no label.

All it takes is one mistake.

The fundamental differences that teeter between a man's paranoia of being with one woman,

and a woman's fear of being betrayed by one man,

is a familiar seesaw battle many endure.

We search for insecurities found,

where trust will eventually have to serve as the guide to commitment.

Alignment.

A man's mind,

heart,

gut instinct,

and lower half of himself,

face the gamut of order women keep their emotions in,

with a better gauge of their chakras.

Beauty fades,

and staying power lies within someone you can grow with,

because quality will always outlast quantity.

I was learning for the first time in my life,

how to center myself to these dynamics because now I held the heart of a woman,

who didn't allow my excuses to house my past relationship issues,

to neighbor her pain—

while protecting the solidarity to my people,

and the Black love my parents set as an example,

through my downplaying of an interracial relationship.

You've seen the white sheets,

slave ships,

animus,

and black fists,

they still exist,

it persists —

genocidal Flint water,

and bullets,

enter black bodies for disposal.

Fears of abandoning my people,

and you simultaneously,

in a place that meant survival of that relationship,

required that we be clairvoyant,

and telepathic,

with each other beyond cultural differences for our symbiotic us against the world endeavor.

We did it throughout the course of years,

through my trepidation —

you yielded to what you didn't know,

and knew enough to learn from what you didn't know,

and truth be told,

the essence of you,

allowed me to take a risk,

outside of my kind that I'm not sure I would take before,

or after you,

with someone not you,

in this society-

because it still refuses to excavate the roots of racism,

due to fear that my people will exact retribution for centuries of heinous oppression.

It never stopped the recognition of my reflection in the soul of a woman not the hue of my skin,

but where I experienced attunement with a partner in a celestial place,

where consciousness precedes color,

a discovery of unconditional love for someone without my blood in their veins.

Montague and Capulet,

in another lifetime,

you were probably my Juliet.

Our halcyon times were the creator's evidence that love is supernatural when fear is absent.

Our turbulent times were evidence of worldly influence and human insecurity when fear is present.

Time has given me the wisdom to know the difference.

You were the mirror I was able to see myself in,

and elevate from the error of my ways,

to heights that seemed reserved for us to meet at,

because the place you would go where no one can reach you,

was once one I retreated to.

Sleight of inhibition convinced me to arrive,

as a visual learner,

in your auditory world,

telling me a million times that you were going to leave,

and didn't sink in until I saw you walk away.

When I feel like I'm losing something,

I fight for it with a frequency that can cool global warming,

and end world wars,

not knowing that a woman is sagacious enough to leave a battle,

long before a man knows there's defeat.

And that every woman since you have pulled you out of my skin,

and their insecurities have followed,

because they see that I'm willing to be alone,

not accompanied by your shadow,

or waiting for you to appear from a silhouette,

but with the resolve that I won't settle for anything less,

than the heights you pushed me to as a better man,

from the kind of connection few people experience during a lifetime.

You didn't believe in coincidence so,

when you uttered the syllables nah-mas-tay,

I always associated my learned meaning with you,

never saw distance between us,

and time really does reveal how you truly feel about someone.

I've written to the subject so many times,

and ways,

not as a hump needed to climb,

to get over you,

but to file a callus only my pencil has been able to pumice.

It's not easy to deem yourself closure when interest is gone,

and people move on so,

these sessions are my medicine.

Requiem for anonymity to the woman who continues to be my greatest ally of alchemy —

I was never more alive than when I gave you everything I had,

to let go of everything I feared I'd lose,

in receiving the true understanding of devotion.

It has taken me listening to silence to know that,

love is honoring mutual autonomy,

and every relationship in our lives requires a continued,

mutual forgiveness

forged through absence,

as the sun is appreciated more when it returns in the morning.

CPSIA information can be obtained
at www.ICGtesting.com
Printed in the USA
LVHW081549041021
699492LV00011B/1511